Table Of Contents

- How I Accidentally Became an App Business Owner
- Things to do BEFORE Making Your First App
- Your App and Business Strategy
- 7 Must Have Items to Start an App Business
- 10 Must Have Resources for the App Business Owner
- Notes on Submitting Apps
- Market Research
- 10 Reasons to Start Selling Mac Apps
- Setting up Your App For the Store
- Marketing without spending money
- App Flipping
- Developing your own apps
- Persistence Pays Off
- Selling an App Business

How I Accidentally Became an App Business Owner

In 2010 I was working as a physicist at a national lab. Running my own business was the furthest thing from my mind - I was making good money, although at times my job was tedious. But then some budget cuts hit - and I got laid off, joining the millions of others who were out of work (and many still are).

Getting laid off from your job is a crushing shock, but I was lucky this time. On a whim doing some hobby type experimentation, I had already posted a few apps for sale in the iPhone app store. To my surprise, they were quickly bringing in significant money. In fact at the time I got laid off they were already bringing in nearly $3,000 a month in profits. My apps were simple but they made regular money, so I figured all I had to do was lather, rinse and repeat to grow my income. My first day off work I headed down to the Apple Store to buy a brand new Mac so I could begin expanding my business. Within a few months of being laid off I was able to replace the income I had been making as a physicist working fulltime. While my life seemed more uncertain, I had control over my time. I could take off and go hiking or whatever, whenever I wanted. I answered to noone except my customers. I could get up as early or as late as I wanted, and it quickly became clear that getting laid off was a blessing in disguise.

Back then the app store was a simpler place. For starters there were a lot fewer apps in the store, and big players were just beginning to take the mobile space seriously. Add to this the fact that the app store allowed for easier app discovery than it does now. These factors created a situation where if you put up a halfway decent app that targeted a niche or was useful, and you were pretty well guaranteed to see at least SOME money from it. When I first started, I was making iPhone apps that only brought in $300-$500 in profit each. But make 10 of those, and you've got a $60,000 a year income. Soon enough I hit on a couple that were making thousands a month, and you get the picture.

Well since then you can sum up the app store with one sentence. Things have changed. The app store is crowded with more than a million apps. Competition between mobile platforms is fierce, and large companies are throwing their weight around the app store. Large app makers are willing to sue independent developers over a trademark infringement claim and unscrupulous developers are willing to copy your work to make a fast buck. On top of swimming with all those sharks, add to that changes Apple constantly makes to the store like removing the "new releases" section, making it harder for apps made by smaller developers to be seen. The end result is you have a mix that's a lot tougher than it was even just a few years ago. But don't be discouraged - despite these changes the app store remains a great business opportunity. With a little preparation and good management, you can build a successful business and maybe even strike it rich.

In the early days even before I got involved it really was a kind of wild west/gold rush atmosphere. You've probably heard about the game iShoot, which made its developer rich in the blink of an eye, as described in a WIRED article:

APPLE'S IPHONE APPLICATION STORE IS AS CROWDED AS A BEYONCE CONCERT, WITH MORE THAN 20,000 APPS AVAILABLE. BUT ONE INDEPENDENT DEVELOPER STILL MANAGED TO RAKE IN $600,000 IN A SINGLE MONTH WITH A SINGLE IPHONE GAME.

These days, with the app store as crowded as the city of Chicago rather than a small Beyonce concert, instant success is going to be harder to grasp. That being said an app business has huge advantages:

- Starting an app business is a low cost endeavor compared to most other types of businesses
- It's easy to retool and bounce back from failures
- It's still a growing market and likely to be for some time
- You can grow your business without investing much if anything in advertising or marketing
- People can't seem to get enough apps, so you can supply them with new ones

The iShoot type of success is still possible - if you're clever enough to come up with a unique idea. But even if you're not, with a little preparation you can build a successful business. Let's get started.

Things to do BEFORE Making Your First App

The app store isn't a game, it's a business. So treat it like one and set up a business before getting stared on anything else. You can set up an individual account with Apple, but that isn't a good idea. A couple of things to consider:

- You might want to sell your app business down the road. If you put your apps in your individual iTunes account, that might cause some sticking points. This isn't as much of an issue as it used to be, since Apple now allows app transfers between accounts. But its still something to consider.

- Legal protection. You wouldn't start any other type of business without considering this angle, so don't treat the app business differently. Yes, you might get sued as a result of running an app business or run into tax trouble (lets hope not of course). So protect your personal assets by creating a company to run the app business.

Setting up your company

Setting up a company is easy. This discussion is limited to working in the USA although there may be similarities elsewhere. As I see it there are basically two choices:

- Limited liability company

- S-corporation

First what are these and how are they different? Let's check Wikipedia.

A limited liability company is a flexible form of enterprise that blends elements of partnership and corporate structures. An LLC is not a corporation; it is a legal form of company that provides limited liability to its owners in the vast majority of United States jurisdictions. ...

1. http://en.wikipedia.org/wiki/Limited-liability_company

Kind of helpful, but also a little bit vague. But what we get out of this is that a limited liability company protects your personal assets. That's what we're after. Beyond this, I found the description on Wikipedia to be somewhat inaccurate, at least as far as the US. They talk about electing to be a S or C corporation, but if you do that you're not an LLC. In the US an LLC is a distinct type of entity that has advantages of simplicity but some slight disadvantages when it comes to taxation. In a nutshell:

- An LLC creates a seperate legal business entity that is not a sole proprietorship or partnership. So it protects your personal assets and you can take on investors for a share of the company.

- Income from an LLC is just passed through to the owners. Basically, you will pay the tax on your share of profits as ordinary income.

The latter point is important. It has two consequences:

- You will pay tax at the higher income tax rate (as compared to capital gains or dividends).

- You will need to save social security and medicare tax to cover your earnings from the business.

According to Turbo Tax, you will be facing:

- 12.4 percent for Social Security. For 2013, this part of the tax applies to the first $113,700 of earnings. If you earn more than that (from self-employment or, if you also have a job, from the combination of your job and your business), then the 12.4 percent part of the tax that pays for Social Security stops for the year.

- 2.9 percent for Medicare. The Medicare portion of the self-employment tax doesn't stop. No matter how much you earn, you'll pay the 2.9 percent Medicare tax. For more information on this tax, see IRS Tax Topic 554: The Self-Employment Tax.

(visit https://turbotax.intuit.com/tax-tools/tax-tips/Self-Employment-Taxes/The-Self-Employment-Tax/INF12023.html for more information).

Setting up your LLC

This isn't a book on starting a business, so I'm not going to go into the details. However setting up an LLC is amazingly simple. It requires a couple of steps:

- Decide what to name your business.
- Go to your states corporation website. Check the availability of your business name. Find the paperwork required to start an LLC.

- Fill out the paperwork, submit with fee.
- The state will mail you a letter or some kind of certificate. Your business is now official.
- Visit a bank with your documents, and open a business checking account.
- When Apple distributes your sales money each month, you can pay it out to yourself and partners as profits or create salaries for yourself (the more complicated option).
- At the end of the year, the LLC will issue a 1099-MISC reporting how much money they paid out to each of the owners. You need to report your 1099 income on your 1040.

Going the Corporation Route Instead

Alternatively, you may wish to create a corporation. I advise taking this route. Its not much more complicated, and at the time of writing at least, offers some advantages. The first thing to know if you don't already is there are two types of corporations:

- S-corporation
- C-corporation

If you just create a corporation, its going to be a C-corporation. That's bad because a C-corporation has to pay its own income tax. So you're going to fall victim to double taxation. The corporation pays income tax, distributes the profits to you, and then you pay tax on the money you receive. Sounds like a bad deal doesn't it?

So what is an S-corporation? For the answer, we again turn to Wikipedia, who tells us:

AN S CORPORATION, FOR UNITED STATES FEDERAL INCOME TAX PURPOSES, IS A CORPORATION THAT MAKES A VALID ELECTION TO BE TAXED UNDER SUBCHAPTER S OF CHAPTER 1 OF THE INTERNAL REVENUE CODE. IN GENERAL, S CORPORATIONS DO NOT PAY ANY FEDERAL INCOME TAXES. INSTEAD, THE CORPORATION'S INCOME OR LOSSES ARE DIVIDED AMONG AND PASSED THROUGH TO ITS SHAREHOLDERS. THE SHAREHOLDERS MUST THEN REPORT THE INCOME OR LOSS ON THEIR OWN INDIVIDUAL INCOME TAX RETURNS.

http://en.wikipedia.org/wiki/S_corporation

So, basically an S-corporation is like an LLC. But it has a huge advantage. When you create an S-corporation you can distribute profits as DIVIDENDS. If you're making a lot of money, this could provide some good tax savings. Of course this is subject to change depending on what the clowns in Washington decide to do with tax rates. But for now, the tax rates are significantly lower than taxes on ordinary income. Moreover, it gives you a way to avoid FICA taxes.

And where the extra income is earned from passive dividends how much extra in FICA and Medicare taxes would they be paying? $0.

Read more about cutting your tax bill with dividends at http://www.financiallyintegrated.com/saving/cut-your-tax-bill-with-dividends/.

Setting up an S-Corporation

At this point, hopefully you've realized creating an S-corporation is the way to go. How do you do that? Follow these steps:

- Pick a name for your business.

- Consider incorporating in Delaware or Nevada to avoid paying some state taxes related to corporations.

- Get on the corporation commission websites and search to make sure your name is available.

- Pay the appropriate fees and submit the appropriate forms.

- It's to your advantage to use a legal service like LEGALZOOM to do this for you. A corporation is required to have certain documents and stock certificates and they not only get the corporation set up for you, they create these required documents.

- When you get your corporation approved and receive the paperwork from the state government and/or legalzoom or other service, issue stock certificates. When you create your corporation you need to declare a certain number of shares. To make it easy, create 100,000. Then issue shares based on ownership percentages. If you have an equal partner issue a stock certificate to each of you with 50,000 shares each. Remember that when the company pays out dividends you each get 50% in that case.

- At the end of the year, your income in this case will be reported by the corporation as ordinary dividend payments on a 1099-DIV.

Now, I am not an accountant or tax advisor. So take this advice as a general description and not actual business or tax advice - and consult the appropriate professional for setting up and managing your business.

A final task BEFORE setting up your Apple developer account is to make sure you have an Employer Identifier Number or EIN for the business. This is basically like a social security number to identify the business.

The Dreaded DUNS Number

OK so you've set up your business. An icky part of creating a business developer account with Apple is at least at the time I am writing this is they require a DUNS number to create the account. In my view, this requirement is fluff and kind of phony, but they require it so if you want to play in the app store you've got to have one. Guess what - a DUNS number is issued by a company called Dun & Bradstreet and while you can get one free, you're probably going to end up paying $500 to get one.

Deal with this BEFORE actually going to create your iTunes account for the business. To do it, visit this website: http://business.dnb.com/

Why will you probably end up paying for it? Well they allow you to get one for free, but it will take 4-5 weeks to get the number. If you pay for it you can get it right away. Seems scammy but that's the way it is. And if you're like me you're going to be anxious to create your Apple account.

Creating Your Developer Account

You are ready to create your Apple Developer Account when you have:

- Created your business
- Have a business checking account
- Have an EIN/Tax number to identify your business (do NOT use your personal SSN or Tax Number)
- Have a DUNS number
- Have a business website
- Have a business email address to use for your Apple ID (keep it separate from your personal Apple ID)
- Have $99-$200 to give Apple

You create your account here: https://developer.apple.com/

Bookmark the website. You're going to be using it a lot, to register new applications and get your certificates.

Why up to $200? Getting an iOS developers account costs $99, and it will allow you to submit iPhone/iPad apps to the store. But the savvy developer also creates Mac apps (see chapter 10 REASONS TO START SELLING MAC APPS). Becoming a Mac developer requires a separate registration and registration fee. Once both are set up, however, you'll access your iOS and Mac stuff from the same account.

The last piece of the puzzle is itunes connect (https://itunesconnect.apple.com/). After registering, and being informed by email from Apple that your account is a go, you need to log into itunes connect to accept your contracts and setup banking information. It's here where you also create new apps (specifically the information that appears in the store, sales copy, screenshots etc.). You also use itunes connect to track your sales and downloads, and apps are submitted to itunes connect. Its also where you go to see if your app is waiting for review etc.

Your App and Business Strategy

Now you're ready to get started. You might have a great idea. Or maybe you're not sure how to proceed. What's the best way forward? The first thing to realize is that betting the farm on a single app is not a great idea. The app store gained some of its magical appeal with stories of people developing an app in their living room over 2-3 days and becoming instant millionaires. This created an all-or-nothing mystique that continues to swirl around the app store.

Some Problems with the App Store

Unfortunately the way the app store is setup encourages this. In my view, Apple has designed the app store very poorly. Only a tiny fraction of the apps that are out there are visible to customers. There are limited sorting options when searching, and the number of categories for apps is extremely limited. Two major weaknesses the app store has include:

- No drill down on generic categories.
- Removal by Apple of the new releases section for non-game apps, in the US store.

To illustrate the first problem, consider the EDUCATION category. If you click on this you're going to see a ton of apps aimed at toddlers. Here and there you'll come across a religious app or an app aimed at college students, but the bulk are kiddie apps.

I've got nothing against apps designed to help kids learn, but having a simple generic education category is limiting the possibilities in the app store. Kiddie apps are crowding out other types of education apps. To see why this is a problem, jump on Amazon.com, and look at how their store is organized. Its much more user friendly and directed at helping the customer find what they want. There is almost an endless ability to drill down into cateogries on Amazon, allowing you to view categories for specific subjects that could fit within education (biology, math, political science, study guides). This helps customers and it also helps those selling books, since you can directly target your audience. The games category is structured differently on the app store, allowing you to target games to say casino, or word/trivia.

To its credit Apple did recently create a kids category, but they need to create sub categories with top selling lists in each one. Until they do, however, we're going to have to live with what the store offers.

The second weakness is the removal of the "new releases" section, which used to allow users to see all apps in a category and sort on release date. Now you're limited to seeing either a tiny set of maybe 20 apps that Apple picks out for you, or the top selling lists (note this is not true for the games category). Many developers claim you shouldn't rely on the new releases section anyway, but the downside is huge - you lose the opportunity to get your app out there directly in front of users for a few days giving it a chance to get some traction and get on a top selling list. In my view the design freaks at Apple believe the store should seem less cluttered, but they aren't looking at it from the customers point of view.

Dealing with the App Store As it is

Apple is unlikely to listen to my complaints so we have to deal with the app store as it is. Fo you this means:

- Creating well designed icons that stand out
- Making great looking screenshots
- Choosing keywords carefully
- Writing SEO copy for your app description

We'll discuss this in detail in SETTING UP YOUR APP FOR THE STORE.

The Overall Business Model

Despite the weaknesses inherent in the app store, its possible to create apps that get on the charts. Here I want to discuss setting goals for the business. A real business is usually not driven off a single hit product. You can do that, but how likely is that? Especially given the way the app store is structured, betting that you're going to create a single app, and its going to rise into the top 10 of its category and make sustained money, that's unlikely.

Our goal is to create a real, sustainable business. Let's look at some existing large businesses. You could consider Walmart or Ford Motor Company for example, and I'll focus on Ford for illustration. Ford does in fact have a couple of flagship products. The F150 Truck is the best selling vehicle in the USA. Ford is also well known for the Mustang.

But if you go to a Ford dealership, its not a lot containing all F150 trucks, there is a wide variety of vehicles. There are many models - the Ford Explorer, Ford Focus, and so on. Ford isn't betting their entire existence on the F150, and they could weather a downturn in F150 sales because they have a large product line. Your app business model should mimic this approach.

In my view, a good approach for most app businesses is to create a wide variety of apps - possibly selling them in different Apple accounts. Let's illustrate this with an imaginary business. So a light bulb went off in your head and you've got what you think is a million dollar app idea. Should you run out and spend $5,000 hiring a developer to make it? Maybe not right away. I would opt for a more conservative approach. We'll set up a new app business that will target the following categories:

- iPhone photo apps
- Slot Machine apps
- A couple of simple lifestyle apps
- A couple of Mac productivity/business apps
- Our one great idea

After doing some research on the photography and lifestyle categories to get ideas (see the chapter on MARKET RESEARCH), set out to see if you can get these ideas off the ground without investing too much into developer resources (see chapter 10 MUST HAVE RESOURCES FOR THE APP BUSINESS). The strategy here is to get your app business going without investing too much time or money so its bringing in a couple of thousand per month. You're not going to impress many friends with this but its going to generate the money you'll need for your one great idea.

A perennial winner in the app store (and in real life) is the slot machine. In the APP FLIPPING chapter we tell you where to get one. Your initial investment is going to cost you between $700-$800 for a slot machine source code. You're also going to have to spend $500-$900 to "reskin" the app (change the theme and graphics). The good news is after your initial investment getting the source code, you can generate multiple slot machine apps by simply changing the graphics, so your costs drop after getting the first app out.

There are two approaches to use with slot machine apps. Most people opt for the fremium model that makes money both from ads and in-app purchases of "coins". My experience is this works pretty well, I've seen $400-$500 in ad revenue per month on an average slot machine game, and maybe another $300 a month for in-app purchases. If you have decent graphics in your reskin, chances are good you'll make back your initial investment in the first month.

Don't stop there. While everyone is obsessed with freemium, PAID IS NOT DEAD. People tend to look at the top grossing list for the app store - which is full of free games, and conclude they need to devote their lives to freemium. But like the real economy, the app store is not a zero sum game. Although free apps are making a greater share of overall app revenue, paid apps are still making money and overall app store revenue is growing. So although paid apps are taking a smaller share of the pie than they used to, the pie is larger.

I've found good success releasing paid slot machine apps as well. The paid category is less crowded, and you benefit by getting users to drop the initial $1.99 or so for the app. In your paid version of the slot machine you still sell "coins" via in-app purchase so will make some money from that as well. The justification for selling a paid slot machine is you remove ads from the app, so you're not bugging the user with ads. This might sound risky but its worked for me - I've made as much from paid slot machines as from free slot machines.

Another benefit is it allows you to leverage the same app source code and graphics. Instead of just releasing one app, you actually release two and double your return on investment.

Let's say to get started you release three slot machine games. Be sure to link them together - and let the user know they can remove ads from the app by paying $1.99. We will discuss approaches to doing this in the chapter MARKETING WITHOUT SPENDING MONEY.

Keep Moving with a Diversified Approach

The past few paragraphs make it seem like you're going to start a slot machines business, but that's not the goal. You should be simultaneously releasing other apps in different categories. The goal here is to get started slowly and not too big to generate some cash that can be used to get your great ideas developed, and hopefully make some money on the side.

So while you're making your slot machine apps, you're also going to be releasing a few apps:

- One or two photo apps. Look on Chupa Mobile or Apptopia to find a pre-built photo app that isn't to expensive, and enhance it in some way to make it more useful to the customer.

- Make a simple lifestyle app. This could be a wallpaper app.

- Create a simple reference app. This can be an app that simply presents some information users are hungry for, like a "cheat" app for a popular game.

Your goals should be two-fold:

- Help generate at least some of the money you need for the app or apps you hope will be big hits.

- Create some base revenue to help you weather downturns.

- Create a diversified portfolio.

In regard to the last point, its like stock investing. Many fools blindly put all their money in a single stock, while financial advisors are yelling "diversify". The same applies here. When your photo apps are sinking, if you're diversified, your slot machine apps or lifestyle apps will be making up for declines elsewhere to help keep you maintaining a steady income.

7 Must Have Items to Start an App Business

The approach I am going to take here - based entirely on experience - is to neglect non-Apple platforms. That isn't to say you shouldn't include Android and even Windows in your app strategy. However, for making money, the iOS app store still remains king. Based on my experience as a four year veteran of the app store wars, the best way to move forward is to establish an Apple oriented business first. Then create Android versions of your apps and consider entering the Windows app store. With that in mind, lets see what tools we need.

1. An iPhone

You may or may not be a developer yourself, but even if you hire someone to create the apps for you, it's very important to have a device to test out the apps on. In addition, you're going to need a device to explore other apps in the store for market research. You're going to want to download apps, use them, and think about how to improve on them while using them on your device, not just looking at pictures on websites and cooking up ideas. So if you're serious about running an app business and don't have an iPhone, get one as soon as possible.

2. An iPad

Some "appreneurs" recommend only developing iPhone apps, but that's foolish. Neglecting the iPad world means neglecting tens of millions of other users that want apps for their iPads. You are going to want an iPad in addition to an iPhone so that you can evaluate the user experience on the iPad as well, and do research in the app store on iPad only apps. You may, for specific applications, also want to develop iPad only apps. The tablet market is exploding so why neglect it? Thinking iPhone only is backward, limited thinking.

3. A Mac computer

A Mac computer is required to develop apps for the app store and submit them to the app store so Apple can sell them for you. So that you're not missing any pieces I recommend getting a recent model Mac of some kind for your business. This is a business - so you should go all in on the Apple ecosystem. While some people like doing their research on an iPhone, a Mac computer makes this much easier. The iTunes app for the Mac computer makes browsing and searching easier, and its also easier to go back and forth between the app store and websites used for research like appshopper.com.

In a future chapter we discuss why you should include making and selling Mac apps as part of your business - so there's another reason to get a Mac. There are many options available, even if you just get a Mac mini or a Macbook Air, you're doing the right thing.

4. Skype

Chances are most readers are not computer software developers. So, you're going to need to hire developers. If you live in the US, Australia, Canada, or Europe, software developers in your local country are going to be too expensive, and if you can avoid it why get tangled up with nasty things like payroll taxes. That means you're probably going to be hiring developers overseas, like from China, India, or Russia. A good developer is going to want to interact with you. So make sure you have Skype installed on your computer for the occasional meeting so you can keep tabs on what they are doing.

5. A Website

Simply put, Apple requires one. For low-cost, easy to use hosting, sign up at Bluehost.com. You will need to have a website where users can contact you for technical support that you submit with each of your apps. Many developers don't put much effort into the website, for now you can just create a single page with an email address that people can use to contact you to ask questions or get technical support.

6. Consider a Blog

Generally, blogs are tedious. But consider writing one where you update your fans about apps your developing and releasing. Write articles about great features in your apps and plans for future apps (that you're willing to reveal of course). If a blog is successful, its a good way to bring in some free web traffic and hence publicity for your apps that you gather outside the appstore.

7. Sign up for app ad services

These days, many people are making money from "freemium". They post free apps in the store that serve ads. I'm not as much of a fan of this, because I'm more interested in giving customers value (and customers will PAY for value) than I am trying to scam them into clicking on ads with a free game. Nonetheless, this approach does offer an opportunity to bring some money in. So as part of your prep for building a successful app business sign up. The best services are applovin.com and revmob.com. Like everything in the app store, the ad world is fast changing. When I first started with it I was making $4,000 a month from one app only using revmob. Now revmob doesn't generate nearly as much, but applovin works pretty well. By the time you read this things might be totally different so do your research.

10 Must Have Resources for the App Business Owner

It's possible to develop apps all by yourself and simply check your iTunes account to try and figure out how things are selling. Unfortunately the way that iTunes Connect presents data is completely haphazard. As a result you're going to want to sign up for a third party service to track app sales and rankings. Here we're also going to explore resources where you can get source codes, developers, graphic artists and other tools required to run an app business. For the record I have no association with the businesses and websites listed below and receive no compensation for recommending them.

1. AppFigures

When you sign up for iTunes Connect and get your first app for sale, you're going to be surprised by their haphazard sales reports. Sales are not grouped together. For example, you'll see sales of a given app for each country listed seperately, but Apple doesn't provide totals. Nor do they give you estimates of how much money is earned, or do conversions to your home currency.

To get around all this a must have tool for an app business is appfigures.com. For a modest charge, you can get your app sales tracked daily with total income and downloads emailed to you each morning. The website provides nice graphs and bar charts of your sales, with flexibility to examine individual apps, selected apps, or all your apps together over any time period. You can view sales by country and track sales ranks in every country where your apps are sold. You can also track sales ranks for all apps in the itunes store and Google Play. I strongly advise creating an appfigures account soon after you've launched your first app in the store. It tracks both mobile and Mac applications.

2. App Annie

For sales charts, nothing beats App Annie. Best of all you can create a free account. App Annie tracks the top 500 apps in the paid, free, and grossing sales lists. You can look at top sales lists for overall or by category. App Annie also tracks sales for iPhone, iPad, Google Play, Amazon.com's Android store, the Mac App Store, and Windows app store. Visit http://appannie.com.

3. oDesk

If you're a computer programmer, you might be developing your own apps. If not you'll need to hire a developer. There are several websites where this can be done, but in my experience oDesk is the best website for hiring workers. When you post jobs you're going to get applications from all over the world. Visit oDesk.com to get started.

elance.com is a close second. There is also Freelancer.com, but I don't like Freelancer.com. It's a kind of loud website that bombards you with stimuli but worst of all it seems to have hidden charges, like a monthly membership fee you get charged even if you're not hiring people. They also go overboard trying to verify you when you attempt to hire somebody, they called me on the phone several times. High pressure salesmanship you can do without by sticking to oDesk.

4. Apptopia

Don't think you need to start app development from scratch. In the past couple of years, a second hand market for app source codes has sprung up, and http://apptopia.com is a good place to browse apps for sale. Many of the apps don't have many downloads but don't let that discourage you. Investigate apps that strike your interest. There can be many reasons why an app didn't sell, it may have poor marketing or bad graphics, or a poorly designed icon. You can jump start your app development by snagging a functional app that needs improvement, and slap some new graphics on it and you're in business. App transfer is easy these days allowing you to immediately buy and app and have it for sale in your account.

5. BlueCloud Solutions

While I generally recommend creating original apps, "reskinning" or "flipping" existing apps (i.e. changing the graphics, icon and theme) can be a part of your business. In fact I've done it myself a few times. This approach is particularly useful when you're developing game apps. A website where you can find high quality app source codes for sale is BlueCloud solutions. They have a great slot machine app, as one example, but also sell occasional utility and camera apps. Visit them at http://www.bluecloudsolutions.com/.

6. Angela's App Services

To reskin a game and actually make money you're going to need good graphics. You can hire your own graphic designers on oDesk or elance.com, but one service you shoudl be aware of is Angela's App Services (http://angelasappservices.com/). This website has graphic designers with lots of app experience and is especially useful if you're looking for new graphics to reskin a game.

7. Screen Taker and Promotee

Having good screenshots is vital for app store success. Using Xcode you can get screen shots directly from a connected device, but often its easier to just grab screenshots from the simulator. An app called screentaker (https://itunes.apple.com/us/app/screentaker/id460043075?mt=12) makes grabbing screenshots from the simulator easy.

Promotee (https://itunes.apple.com/us/app/promotee/id578071639?mt=12) lets you put your screen shots on great looking device images, including iPhone, iPad, Mac, and Android devices. The images created with Promotee look completely professional.

8. Other Developer Tools in the Mac App Store

Open the Mac App Store periodically and check the DEVELOPER TOOLS category. Most of the apps for sale there tend to be for web developers, but there are several aimed at mobile developers that you might find useful.

9. Chupa Mobile and Code Canyon

Revisiting the reskinning theme, if you're looking more for non-game apps visit Chupa Mobile (http://www.chupamobile.com/ios) and Code Canyon (http://codecanyon.net/category/mobile/ios). You can save time and money by picking up app templates from these websites. For example, if you have an idea for a radio app, you can pick up a radio app template and hand it off to your developer. Since the app is already half developed, you can save money by only paying the developer half of what they'd normally charge. Let's say for a radio app your developer would charge you $1800. You could pick up a radio app on Chupa Mobile for anywhere from $21(http://www.chupamobile.com/products/details/391/RadioStream/) to a few hundred. Then pay your developer to finish it to your specifications for just $900, saving a bunch of money.

10. App Mockup Software

Another way to save time and money is to get an app mockup app. This will allow you to design your screens and app flow. Dapp is a leader (https://itunes.apple.com/us/app/dapp-app-creator-make-learn/id370888555?mt=8). Another useful tool in this category is iMockup(https://itunes.apple.com/us/app/imockups-for-ipad/id364885913?mt=8).

Notes on Submitting Apps

One of the most stressful parts of running an app business for most people is dealing with the app submission process and Apple. However, its important to not let this get to you. Getting all worked up over a rejected app is a sign of immaturity not suitable to a successful business owner.

First a few facts. Apple controls the store and they run the show. Accept that and move on. Here is how it basically works.

- You submit an app uploading it with Xcode (or having your developer do that for you).

- If you've done everything correctly, it will change to WAITING FOR REVIEW.

- The waiting for review step takes on average 7 days. Sometimes it goes faster, sometimes slower, but the 7 day rule is a good rule of thumb.

- Knowing that it takes 7 days, after your app goes into Waiting For Review, forget about it and move on to a new task. Fretting over when it will get reviewed is a complete waste of time and energy.

- When an app goes IN REVIEW, it typically takes 8-10 hours. Sometimes it goes really fast, and sometimes it takes longer like 24 hours. Again, worrying about it is a waste of your time and energy.

When the review process is complete, you will receive an email. If your app was approved for sale, you will receive a notice that its *Processing for the App Store.* You will receive a second email a couple of hours later saying that the app is READY FOR SALE. It takes some time (often up to a day) for the app to actually show up on the store. So don't waste time and energy continually checking the store to see if its there. If you're submitting a game app (which still has a new releases section), the app will show up in your developer's account app listing in the store before it shows up in new releases a few hours later. At that point, you're in business.

The Dreaded App Rejection

An app rejection is not the end of your life - so deal with it without getting hysterical. If you search the internet you're going to see that many app developers flip out over an app rejection. Again, that's a waste of time and energy.

Rejections come in various flavors. The first one isn't quite a rejection. It's the dreaded YOUR APP REQUIRES ADDITIONAL REVIEW TIME email. In this case, the initial reviewer has seen something that requires a look by someone higher up or more specialized, so your app gets kicked to a different reviewer. A common cause of this is:

- Using graphics or music you don't have copyright or right to use

- Using a name or phrase in your app name or description that is trademarked

These are common reasons for more review time, but not all cases are described by these situations. If your app is requiring more review time for these reasons, it's going to get rejected.

Often, additional review time means there is a technical issue. In one case I had removed ads from an app but had left the ad serving frameworks in the app. I was instructed to remove these and resubmit the app.

Not all APP REQUIRES ADDITIONAL REVIEW TIME cases will be rejected, so don't make that assumption. Also, time required can range from a day to more than a month. Sorry but that's the way it is. Sitting around stressing out over it is another waste of time and energy - so take care of other tasks related to your business while you're waiting to hear about the approval or rejection.

When an app is rejected, they will direct you to the RESOLUTION CENTER. Log into itunes connect, and then open the page for the app (going to the app details page). There you'll see the resolution center which will tell you why the app was rejected. If they think you don't have rights for graphics or music but you do and can document it, you can submit proof here. It will probably take some time for them to get back to you. It's also possible to submit an appeal to the "app review board" here. I tried that once, and didn't have much luck.

Often an app will be rejected for METADATA. This means you just have to change the app title, keywords, screen shots, or text description of the app. For example suppose you had created an app called *MixItUp with The Beatles.* Now, obviously "The Beatles" is trademarked, so you can't use it in your app title. If you app name (on the binary) is MixItUp, a metadata change request would probably entail changing the title to MIXITUP - UNOFFICIAL EDITION FEATURING THE BEATLES. The change seems trivial but Apple is picky about not giving users the impression that you're associated with a given product, group, or service. They also might make you remove trademarked words that you're using as keywords, or change screenshots that include copyrighted material.

In a metadata change you don't have to actually recompile and submit your app again, you just make the metadata change and click "Submit new metadata". Your app goes back to "Waiting for

Review", but usually in these cases the app will go back into review and get approved in a day or two.

If your binary is rejected, you will have to fix the problem, resubmit and go to the end of the line. Unfortunately its like starting over from scratch, so plan on waiting up to a week before its reviewed again.

The key to surviving all this is to remember you're running a business. You're thinking long term, and the lifetime of the app might be several years. So a couple of weeks getting it submitted for sale is trivial.

A few tips to avoid rejection

Sometimes Apple's decisions seem arbitrary and capricious. However most of the time its not - follow the rules to avoid rejection. A few key tips:

- Don't submit pornographic images. We can complain about Apple being uptight, but its their store and they create the rules. You know what they are ahead of time so follow them before creating apps.

- Read the HUMAN INTERFACE GUIDELINES provided on developer.apple.com. Apple lays their rules out for you. Read it and familiarize yourself with the rules, and this will help you avoid rejections.

- Don't use others copyrighted images, either in your app or in your metadata.

- Avoid using trademarked words or phrases in your app title or keywords. Hoping to get app traffic using them is scammy anyway. Make money by providing value for your customers, not by trying to scam them into buying your app with cheap search tricks.

- If you create an app relying on a famous game or person, make it clear that the app is "unofficial". Use the term unofficial in your app title and description. Don't use the person or games name in your app name (i.e. create PHOTO FAN APP - JUSTIN BEIBER EDITION, not JUSTIN BEIBER PHOTO FAN APP).

- Don't try to collect user information on the device using UDID

- Don't spam the store. You can create multiple slot machine or poker apps, but Apple frowns on releasing the same utlity app ten times.

- Avoid using foul language or realistic graphic violence.

- If you use third party libraries, check to ensure that they are compliant.

We can't forsee all reasons for app rejection, but following these basic rules will help you avoid a great deal of rejections. If your app does get rejected, don't flip out and give up, just do what they request and resubmit.

Market Research

We all have our great ideas, and chances are you're coming to the app business with a great idea you think is going to make you rich. Well it might or it might not, but in any case, doing market research is important in the app business as it would be for any type of business. Luckily its pretty easy to do.

Study the Marketplace

Studying the market place means taking time to see what's going on in the app store. You can do this on your phone, the iPad, or on your desktop computer using the iTunes app. Another useful resource for this purpose is http://appshopper.com. I like looking at this website because they keep a record of price changes for each app.

Why is this important? An app that has hundreds of reviews can be deceptive. If you see an app that costs $2.99 and it has a hundred reviews, that's a good indication that the app is making great money and has lots of users. On the other hand, if the developer made the app free for a week, they might have gotten all those reviews from free users, so maybe the app isn't making as much money as you think. So you'll want to use appshopper as a cross check for this purpose. An app that has a large number of reviews that hasn't been offered as free is one that has more value.

The main way to get to know your marketplace is to study the top paid, free, and grossing lists on the app store. You're only going to want to study the top 50 selling apps. In most categories apps that aren't in the top 50 aren't making that much money. That doesn't mean if you get an app ranked 120 say on the lifestyle category, that for you its not making money - it might be making $60 a day. But when researching to come up with app ideas, we want to focus on the top sellers.

Three things to keep in mind:

- Spend time studying the app store. Devote some time each day to see what is selling.

- Watch for trends. If you suddenly see a new type of app shoot up the charts, it could be an opportunity to capitalize. Example - a few months prior to writing this book, "monogram" wallpaper apps suddenly started showing up in the top 10 list for the lifestyle category.

- Look for sustainable apps. Some types of apps are evergreen sellers.

A great resource for studing the appstore is http://www.distimo.com/iq. Read their blog including the year in review (http://www.distimo.com/blog/2013_12_publication-2013-year-in-review/) and look up data on which app store categories are the most popular.

App Localization

Remember the US isn't the only big market out there. It is worth your time to also study other large markets, in particular Japan. Yes there is a language barrier but you can overcome that with some outsourcing. There may be apps popular in Japan that are not in the US and vice versa - its another opportunity to make more money.

What To Do With your Info

Let's create a systematic procedure for studying the app store, rather than just sitting down and looking at the apps. The goal is to create a new app that leverages top selling apps already in the app store.

1. Begin by choosing a category

Begin by deciding what type of app you want to develop. An entertainment app? Photography app? Or maybe a book app?

2. Look at that category and study which apps are in the top 50. Write down a few that catch your eye. Write down the app name, and 3-4 key features of the app. Do this for 5-7 apps.

3. Buy or download the apps. Free apps, of course, are a great way to approach this. Keep your eye out for free apps that could be improved upon with new features - you could do this and release a new app in the paid category.

4. For each app, note 2-3 flaws of features you wish the app had.

5. Revisit the app listing in the store. Go to the reviews section, and read the reviews. Select MOST CRITICAL. The app store customer base provides a wealth of information - see what users are complaining about or wishing for. Then give it to them.

6. After studying your five apps, reduce it to a single app you can develop right now. Your app should take in the best features of the app you're looking at, and then address its weaknesses or add 1-2 new key features.

By approaching the app store this way, you're taking a more conservative approach more likely to result in success. Looking at the top selling charts to find apps that are already working will help ensure there is a market for your apps.

But, there are already apps doing that

In business a common objection from people is that someone is ALREADY doing that. They will say to you why bother? Someone beat you to the idea.

This is a huge mistake.

If there is an app ALREADY doing X, and the app is in the top 20 or top 50 of the sales charts, that indicates that a market exists for X. People already want it. And chances are, you can spot weaknesses, complaints, or pinpoint features the existing app is missing that users want.

Give the users what they want - and they will download your app.

Often, users will buy multiple apps of the same type. This is similar to books. For example, what if someone made the argument that someone already wrote a weight loss book? Why bother with that? Wrong. People reading weight loss books are likely to buy multiple weight loss books. And, they are certianly going to be interested in buying a new weight loss book that has new ideas and insights. The same principle applies to apps.

As an example consider monogram wallpaper apps. This app has occupied a top 5 position in the lifestyle category for some time:

https://itunes.apple.com/us/app/monogram-wallpaper-backgrounds/id647594931?mt=8

Does that mean nobody else should make monogram apps? NO - it means the opposite - it means YOU should make a monogram app as a way to start generating some steady income. If you study the lifestyle category for any length of time you're going to see several monogram apps in the rankings. Get the top selling app and see how it could be improved. Add your improvements and if you set up your app icon, screenshots, keywords and description right, you will have a money maker on your hands.

10 Reasons to Start Selling Mac Apps

While most app developers are focused or should I say obsessed with mobile apps - the savvy business person utilizes the Mac App Store as a significant part of their business plan. The desktop isn't dead, and despite pronouncements to the contrary, the reality is that computer users are not going to replace their laptops, notebooks, and desktops with iPads. At the time of writing, the future of the Windows 8/8.1 app store is still too uncertain, so I'm going to ignore it for now, but you'll want to keep it in mind for future expansion. In the meantime, start expanding your app plans to include development specifically for the Mac.

To sell apps for the Mac, you can use the same developer account but you'll need to also register as a Mac developer. So that means paying Apple another $99. Your Mac and iOS apps will be available through the same iTunes account, but App IDs and provisioning profiles are managed seperately.

With those notes, let's see why the smart app business develops apps for the Mac and iOS app stores.

1. Desktop apps sell for a premium

Mobile apps are usually free, or 99 cents. At the most they go for something like $2.99, and many users are going to balk at such an expensive price. Developers hope to reach a large number of customers in order to strike it rich.

In contrast, desktop apps can sell for anywhere from $10 up to hundreds and even thousands of dollars, depending on how specialized they are. As a result you don't need to sell very many copies to make real money. In my own app businesses, I've had Mac Apps that only sell 5-10 copies a day that bring in more than $100,000 a year. Some developers are fools - they develop Mac apps and try selling them for 99 cents or a couple of bucks - but studying the top grossing lists you'll see that this is not a winning strategy. Let's take a look at a few examples.

Productivity and business oriented apps are always great for desktop applications. Here is a construction cost estimator. It sells for $39.99 and offers several in-app purchases that are $49.99 each. At the time I'm writing this, the app is ranked #14 in the Business category - so you can see right away this is a good model for making serious money.

Business and personal scheduling and time management apps do well in the Mac Store. For example this calendar app is ranked in the top 5 of the Business category, and sells for $49.99.

To charge more than $20 and so make great money, your app doesn't have to be overly complicated. It just has to be useful. So start studying the Mac App Store and brainstorming.

2. Mac Apps have greater exposure

The iOS app store has a million apps in it. Unless you're selling a game, there is no "new releases" section to give new apps exposure. In contrast, there are not nearly as many apps in the Mac App Store, and the Mac App Store still includes a "new releases" section. Apple allows you to to place your apps in two categories, and it shows up in the "new releases" section of both categories, giving it even more exposure. Since the Mac App Store isn't as hopping as the iPhone/iPad app store, your app will stay at the top of the "new releases" section longer, giving it more chance to get traction and get on a best selling list.

3. Mac Apps allow you to build a customer base across all of Apple's devices

The smartest strategy is to build an app that people will want to use on all their devices. Users that have bought iPhones and iPads are going to migrating from Windows PCs to Macs. Having an app that users need and can install on their iPhone and iPad AND their Mac is a great way to build a solid customer base. In fact you can exploit the increased visibility of the Mac App Store to drive sales of your iPhone and iPad apps. Consider building apps that store data in the cloud and you can create a suite of apps that allow users to work on the same data on their Mac, their iPad, and their iPhone.

4. The Mac App Store has a more diversified app base

If you check the overall top selling and grossing lists on the iPhone/iPad stores, you're going to see tons of games. Other apps - although many are making great money- are way down on the list. In the Mac App Store the top grossing list is pretty surprising. There are hardly any games. This provides an opportunity for developers of productivity, business, and other types of apps.

5. Freemium doesn't reign supreme

The app store in my view has decayed in a race to the bottom. Since you couldn't cut prices from 99 cents, developers began going free and trying to make money from ads or in-app purchases. While you can do that, in my view its going to be iffy for the vast majority of developers. The paid model remains supreme in the Mac app store, allowing you to make money upfront without having to harass and annoy your users with ads.

6. Diversity leads to more stability in income

Creating a business that depends on one income source isn't the smart way to go. Your first impulse is going to be to create Android versions of your iPhone apps, and that might be an important leg in your business. But it is foolish to not make Mac versions of your iPhone apps - and experience shows you're more likely to make money from Mac versions of your apps than you are from Android versions (but not saying you shouldn't also target the Android platform). When you have diversity you'll be better situated to weather the inevitable ups and downs that confront your business. When your iPhone apps see their sales drops, you'll have a buffer with your independent Mac apps, and vice versa.

7. Build Extra Value

The tech world is fast changing and the mobile app space changes even faster. As a result you need to be thinking of an exit strategy so you can cash out before its too late. A more diversified business that shows income from multiple sources is going to be more valued by business buyers, and command a higher selling price.

8. Its Easier to Establish a Brand

Since the Mac App Store is smaller, indie developers are more visible. If you create a suite of apps in the Mac App Store you can create a brand presence in the store seen by millions of customers. Use it to sell more apps in the Mac App Store but also to springboard apps in the iPhone/iPad app store.

9. The Mac share of the computer/pc market is growing

While general PC sales are stagnant and even in decline, and customers complain about the boondoggle of Windows 8, the Mac continues to increase its share of the desktop market. Developing some Mac apps lets you ride this trend.

10. Take Advantage

Take advantage of an opportunity 90% of mobile developers are ignoring in their quest for the iPhone gold rush.

Setting up Your App For the Store

Now you've made a great app. Are you done? No. Your app store entry is as important as the app itself. Your app store entry will include:

- The app icon
- Screenshots of the app
- A text description of what the app does
- keywords for the app

Each of these items is vitally important. Because of changes in the ways that apps are displayed, the icon isn't as important as it used to be, but its still vitally important to have a nice looking app icon. The key features you're shooting for are:

- Good looking professional design
- Clarity - it should be a sharp high resolution image
- An app icon that stands out
- If possible, have the icon communicate what the app does

Making ScreenShots

The first screenshot of your app shows up when people are looking at apps that they've searched for.

So your first screenshot should look the best, and communicate some feature of the app.

Like looking at apps themselves, its a good idea to study the app store to see what successful apps are doing in regard to their screenshots. Screenshots for non-game apps should include:

- images of iPhone or iPad devices
- A quality screen shot or two from your app
- A nice background
- Some text describing a feature of the app

For example - check out https://itunes.apple.com/us/app/emoji-emoticons-for-ios-7/id444304133?mt=8

For game apps, you might want to omit the device shots and directly show a shot of the game. But depending on the type of game you are selling, look at the top 10 selling games of similar type and see what they are doing and duplicate it.

Always duplicate without copying. Write your own sales copy. Make your screenshots similar, but not copies.

A great resource for the do-it-yourself crowd is *Promotee*, a Mac app that lets you put your screen shots on device images that look very professional. You can get Promotee here: https://itunes.apple.com/us/app/promotee/id578071639?mt=12

You can also find someone on oDesk or elance to make screenshots for you. Hire someone that has previous examples to show you. Its relatively inexpensive, you can probably get great screenshots made for you for around $100-$150.

Making an Icon

If you want to design an icon yourself, using either Photoshop or Gimp, make a 1024 x 1024 image. You can then export it as a PNG file. Then get this app ICONS from the Mac App store:

https://itunes.apple.com/us/app/icons/id413612688?mt=12

Icons will create all the icons you need for your app, allowing you to round the corners just right. But again, the best bet is to spend $100 and hire someone on oDesk with experience to make an icon for you.

Keywords

Since Apple got rid of the "new releases" section, keywords have increased in importance. You want good keywords so that users can find your app in the store. Apple lets you enter 100 characters. A tip: don't separate keywords with spaces, use single commas. In other words don't enter keywords as:

monogram, wallpaper, polka dot, design

Enter the keywords like this:

monogram,wallpaper,polka dot,design

Apple counts the spaces as a character, so you might end up being able to add an extra keyword or two by leaving unnecessary spaces out.

Since you only have 100 keywords, choose them carefully. Begin by thinking about what words or phrases users might type in to search for an app of the type you're offering. But you don't have to rely entirely on guesses or hunches.

One useful resource is GOOGLE TRENDS. Check Google trends to see what sorts of things people are searching on.

http://www.google.com/trends/

Another important tool you can use from Google is the Keyword planner. You can enter a word or phrase, and Google will tell you how many people are searching for it on google, but more importantly tell you what related words or phrases its users are also searching for.

https://adwords.google.com/keywordtool

It's designed for Adwords, but is still useful for doing keyword research for your apps.

A final useful tool is Amazon.com. If you search on Amazon.com, notice that when you type in a word or phrase, a drop down list will open showing suggestions. This can help you tease out what related words or phrases customers are using in their searches. Amazon is parituclarly useful since you can do this using both the bookstore and the Android app store.

App Description

The app description is the last part of the puzzle. One thing to remember about the app description is that in the mobile world, users are scanning app entries quickly and often making impulse buys. So it can be helpful to make the first sentence of your app description a straightforward single sentence that clearly states what the app does.

Many top selling apps include notes that their app is the top selling app in seven countries or whatever, or got recognized by Apple or received an award. They do this for social promotion. People are more likely to buy something that has already been approved by their peers. But as a new developer, you don't have that option. So make your first sentence for now basic and straight forward.

"My Great App is an app that does X"

I also like to skip a line and then begin the rest of the app description rather than hitting the customer with a long block of text. So what to include in your text? Features and BENEFITS. Tell the user not just what the app does, but how its going to make their life better, easier etc. Take some time to read these articles about writing sales copy and features vs. benefits:

http://www.entrepreneur.com/article/34942

http://www.ideacrossing.org/blog/index.php/2012/07/why-features-tell-but-benefits-sell/

http://www.inc.com/welcome.html?destination=http://www.inc.com/geoffrey-james/how-to-sell-value-benefits-or-features.html

Marketing without spending money

In my view spending money to market apps is not a way to go for the indie app developer. Large corporations have money to throw away on that, you probably don't, and paying for pay by click ads can lead to serious financial obligations if you're not careful.

That being said, the app store itself provides opportunities to market without spending a dime.

Linking apps together

Don't just put apps out there and hope they sell. If you have 5or 6 apps in the store, you're goign to want to tell your customers about all of them.

One way to do this is to create a "more" or info screen in your app, which is a table displaying your app icons and app names. Create your table to have two lines of text:

- A bold line with the app title.
- A second line below it that states what the app does.

Use the image property of the table cell to prominently display the app icon. If the user taps on the entry, have it take them directly to the app store where they can download it.

Leverage Free Apps

Create free apps in your portfolio, with the purpose of driving traffic to your paid apps. This can be utilized in two ways.

- Create free, and paid versions of your app. Use the free app to encourage users to buy your paid app to get more features. Keep in mind Apple requires free apps to be fully functional apps in their own right.

- Drive traffic to related apps that aren't paid versions of your free app. Example, create a Justin Beiber fan book app that you sell for $2.99. Then create a Justin Beiber fan wallpaper app that's free. The free wallpaper app can be ad supported, but also use it to advertise your own app, the book app that some users will probably want to buy. You already know they are interested in Justin Beiber.

Nag Screens

If you sign up for Revmob, Chartboos or Applovin, you will notice they sell other apps by popping up a screen with good graphics and a prompt to the user to download the app. OK it works for them, it might work for you too. This kind of pop up is called a "nag screen". Create a nag screen to nag the user into downloading your own paid apps. You can have it work like Revmob, have it popup each time the user opens the app. I don't like to pester users of paid apps, but it is appropriate to put this kind of screen in a free app used to drive traffic.

Create multiple app companies to focus on particular types of apps

If a customer likes one of your apps, they are likely to see what other apps you're offering in the store. While you might be developing a wide variety of different app types, consider putting them in different Apple accounts. Suppose for example that you have 3 slot machine apps, a poker app, a photo app, and a font app.

- Create an Apple account for the slot machine app and the poker app. Then when they look to see what other apps you've developed, they'll immediately see more casino apps they are already interested in.
- Do the same for the photo app and font app.

This isn't a strict requirement, but can be helpful if you're putting out apps that are of wildly different types.

Use Local or Push Notifications

A local or push notification is a way to have your app send your users a message. Talk to your developer about actually implementing, but consider sending messages to your users when you release a new app, including a link to the app store.

Leverage across stores

Earlier I advised that you create Mac apps as well. Create Mac apps that are related to your iPhone/iPad apps. Then prompt users of your Mac apps to download your iPhone/iPad apps, and vice versa.

App Flipping

In the introduction I indicated I got started using a "lather, rinse, repeat" approach to growing the business. This wasn't the ONLY way I grew my business, but when you see a particular idea working on one niche, chances are it will work on another niche as well.

Early on, I got some decent success selling wallpaper apps. When I first learned how to create an app, it was easy to display a gallery of images and let the user save them as their iPhone background. Being a horse owner I started with a simple horse wallpaper app. Believe it or not the app got 300,000 downloads. Then it occurred to me to simply swipe out the images and call the app something else. The possibilities are endless - surfing, motorcycles, sports cars, anything people want to stare at related to their hobbies. At one point I made an app that had wallpapers for the boy band One Direction that got more than a million downloads. Each app was the same source code, I just swapped out the images used for the wallpapers, changed the app name and icon, and resubmitted to the store.

This type of approach isn't limited to wallpaper apps. In fact the best category for app flipping is games. People can't get enough of games and probably never will. Taking a successful game and creating a new theme for it with new graphics is an easy way to add to your app portfolio by flipping/reskinning. For example, slot machines are very popular in the app store. At the time of writing there are 12 slot machine games in the top grossing list for iPad games. Slot machines are addictive. Apple isn't picky about letting slot machine game after slot machine game into the app store. Moreoever, you can quickly buy a slot machine code (http://www.bluecloudsolutions.com/source-codes/party_slots_b/). Once you have the slot machine code, you can reskin it 10, 20 times to get multiple games in the store and make money. You pay once up front to get the code, and after that only have to invest in the graphics.

My approach to running an app business is to avoid "putting all your eggs in one basket", so I tend to have multple approaches going at once. Reskinning slot machine games shouldn't be your only way to try and make money in the app store, but should be ONE PART of an overall strategy.

Developing your own apps

Most app business owners are going to hire developers on oDesk. Even if you're a programmer, you're probably going to want to do that as well. Why spend your days and nights toiling with c language at your computer and getting headaches? Let someone else do it, I say.

But if you love developing or want to save money at least at first, you might develop your own apps. I confess I did that and still do some of the time.

To develop your own apps you will need:

- A Mac computer
- Xcode
- To know how to code using c,c++ and more specifically, objective-c
- There are other options, like Game Salad, but you're best off sticking to the tools Apple provides

Xcode is Apple's IDE/Development platform. The language its setup to primarily use is objective-c. You can get Xcode for free here:

https://itunes.apple.com/us/app/xcode/id497799835?mt=12

Xcode will come with "simulators" for the iPhone and iPad you can use while testing your apps.

Developing your own apps is very time consuming and can be frustrating, so I don't really recommend it. But if you insist on forging ahead, you can look at these resources:

Objective-c programming:

http://www.amazon.com/Objective-C-Programming-Ranch-Guide-Guides-ebook/dp/B00GSRITM0/ref=sr_1_1?s=books&ie=UTF8&qid=1391545445&sr=1-1&keywords=objective+c

iOS 7 Programming Fundamentals:

http://www.amazon.com/iOS-Programming-Fundamentals-Objective-C-Basics-ebook/dp/B00FT7KW3Y/ref=sr_1_1?s=books&ie=UTF8&qid=1391545471&sr=1-1&keywords=ios+7+programming

iOS 7 App Development Essentials:

http://www.amazon.com/iOS-7-App-Development-Essentials-ebook/dp/B00FPT5BKK/ref=pd_sim_b_3

And of course my own book:

http://www.amazon.com/dp/B00HLSR8UE

Persistence Pays Off

Your life in the app store is probably not going to be all roses and cashing checks.

You're going to have setbacks.

You're going to post apps that get no downloads. You're going to have app rejections.

So here just a quick note - don't give up so easily. Many developers think they have that great app idea, post it, and it doesn't sell. So they chalk up their app store experience to failure and move on.

To be successful in the app store, chances are you're not going to make it on a single app. So if you post an app that doesn't sell try again. Just don't give into instanity, i.e. doing the same thing over and over and expecting different results.

Make adjustments. Study to see why your app may have failed to gain traction. After you make changes, release a new app.

If you have a paid app that bombed, release a free version that points to the paid app, or put out improved but related apps that encourage users to download the original app. It is possible to revive app sales.

The bottom line though, is one or two failures don't mean you should give up. You might release 20 apps and make 80% of your revenue from just 4-5 of them (the famous 80/20 rule).

Selling an App Business

One thing that's constant about the mobile space is change. Things that take 5 years in other businesses will happen in 12 months in the app sphere. The technology is evolving fast - and Apple's management of the app store is always subject to change. Its going to be hard to start an app business and stay on top of it for the long term and have it keep making money.

That being said one of the best things about app businesses is well, its all virtual. You can create a money making business with 20 apps and then start an entirely new app business wth 20 new apps.

One way to maximize your profitability is to sell off your older app business when you're ready. The best place to do this is http://appbusinessbrokers.com. They are a professional outfit that has experience selling mobile app businesses and websites, and they have many contacts so can hook you up with a buyer ready to take over your app business.

Like everything else associated with the app store, selling app businesses began with a frantic frenzy reminiscent of the California gold rush. People were willing to come in and drop major money, paying up to 24 times annual revenue to grab hold of a profitable app business. Unfortunately for us things have slowed down and matured since then, and people are more cautious. Even so you can cash out selling your app business. At this time you can probably expect to sell it at about 2 times your annual revenue.

So the first key is to get your business on a track to success, so that its actually worth something.

The app business is a lot more casual than other types of businesses, so you're not going to need a whole lot to sell the business. Teams of accountants are not going to show up at your office to go over your records. However you still need to show what you've got, and you'll need to have the following:

- A record of your previous app sales. AppFigures is perfect for this, so you can produce graphs of total sales and individual apps for the buyer.

- 6-12 months of bank statements, showing Apple actually making deposits to your account.

- A simple but accurate profit and loss statement, showing the previous 12 months of expenses and profit.

It's also possible to sell off individual apps. If you need to raise money for more app development, feel you've gotten all you're going to out of a given app or want to cash out on an asset but not the entire business, consider listing individual apps on http://apptopia.com.

Regardless of which path you take, selling at the top of performance is the best time to sell. You don't want to be trying to get someone to take over your app business if it shows income declining every month, so if you're going to list it for sale take some steps to get revenue up when buyers will be looking at it (release new apps etc.).

www.ingramcontent.com/pod-product-compliance
Lightning Source LLC
Chambersburg PA
CBHW071812170526
45167CB00003B/1280